Gary,

A very nice Pr who is very fair to the ministry. God continues to let use you. I love you + your family.

Brenda
09/01/18

Poems On Occasion

A Gift From God

by

Brenda A. Lasenby

authorHOUSE

1663 LIBERTY DRIVE, SUITE 200
BLOOMINGTON, INDIANA 47403
(800) 839-8640
www.authorhouse.com

First published by AuthorHouse 6/14/04

ISBN: 1-4184-5903-8 (e)
ISBN: 1-4184-2101-4 (sc)

Printed in the United States of America
Bloomington, Indiana

This book is printed on acid-free paper.

TABLE OF CONTENTS

A Loosed Woman

Today I stand proud as the Woman I was created to be
I stand loosed from all my shackles - I stand here totally free
I have been beautifully made in God's sight
I have a reason to rejoice and I certainly have a right.

No longer shall we as Women sit and be silent in the church
While souls are out there bound, lost and hurt
Let us go forth and find our place
For time is growing short - we must make haste.

There is something for each and every one of us to do
The sixty-six books of the Bible were written for us too
We strive to raise our children from infants to adults
Sometimes despite our best efforts we obtain negative results.

Hold your head up and know that you are not the blame
Be set free from all your guilt, suffering and pain
Perhaps you are married and are a loving and devoted wife
But know that there is yet more for you in this life.

Who can find a virtuous Woman - to her husband she is a crown
A Woman with good values is not so easily found
Who can find a virtuous Woman - her price is high above rubies
She is not lacking in performing her responsibilities and duties.

You are to be obedient, be fruitful and multiply
But also know your every need the Lord will supply
In the natural, as well as spiritually, we are known as a helpmeet
Our prayers go up to the Father's throne to conquer and defeat.

To say your purpose in this world is not a necessity would be amiss
Without the creation of the Woman, the man child would not even exist
Together with Man, we were put on this earth to work as one
Fighting the bands of the wicked until the day is done.

Women's Day - November 11, 2001

Brenda A. Lasenby

A MOTHER

A Mother's travail in bringing forth is only the beginning
From that point on her care and concerns are never ending
She will nurture, discipline, protect and instruct
At bedtime she ensures that her baby is safely tucked.

One of the greatest joys of all is that of a Mother giving birth
Honor your Mother and Father to have long life on the earth
It has been said that a Mother's job is never done
Attempting to raise "respectable children" is the most important one.

A Mother should create a pathway her offspring can follow
Standards of high morals that are not empty and hollow
Do as I say? -- But not as I do?
Be that good example for their hero lies within you.

The value of a Mother is priceless and cannot be compensated for
She is filled with words of wisdom that you should not ignore
A Mother's instills sound training and from it they will not depart
Though he or she may stray away – they won't go very far.

The disobedience and indifferent behavior a Mother sees
Becomes a burden that keeps you on your knees
All your prayers and endeavors will not be in vain
Nor the sleepless nights that cause so much pain.

When the age of adulthood has been reached
They begin to recall all the sermons Mother has preached
How she encouraged you to prepare and develop a master plan
The direction of your future now lie in your hands.

A Mother may not receive full glory until that first grandchild comes along
It is then she begins to see her "parenting techniques" are being driven home
The reality of parenthood to that son or daughter is becoming a lot clearer
They now visualize their reflection in that mirror.

Mother's Day – 5/11/03

A NEW DAY

I never thought it would happen to us
Things grew worse the more we fussed
I feel the situation within itself is not my fault
But you and I stand in naught.

The stress and the pain has taken its toll
Many years of anxiety has begun to unfold
Though I may feel life is unfair
God knows the count of every hair.

You are not home to hear the telephone when it rings
I alone bear the problems that a single day brings
Let this experience be a lesson to us both
We are to wear the garment of life as a cloak.

Yes, it's sad as sad can be, but
it's not too late for you and me
No, not all has been lost
But are you ready to pay the cost?

We must be willing to work it out
And ask the Creator to take away all doubt
If we can believe, this he can do
It is no telling what awaits me and you.

Starting all over can be scary
Blessings are not from the good fairy
Let us trust in the giver of life
Forgiving each other for all the strife.

Together we can begin a new day
Putting our differences far away
For now is the time for us to say
It does not have to always be done my way.

Brenda A. Lasenby

AN EXPRESSION OF WELCOME

I would like to extend a warm Welcome to all our Guest tonight
Your decision to come was absolutely right!
Whether you are family, an acquaintance or a friend
We're so happy you chose this church to worship in.

Now the Spirit of the Lord is here to set the captive free
And where the spirit of the Lord is - there is liberty
We're so blessed you came out to celebrate with us
But let me warn you - - we keep up a lot of fuss.

We want you to shout, jump and raise your hands
Oh yes, and please don't hesitate to do the holy dance
The minute you walked through our doors
You were not a stranger to us anymore.

Once again, you are Welcome in this holy place
For in the temple you will find peace and you will find grace
We don't believe in just looking around and standing mute
You can feel free to worship the Lord in spirit and in truth.

It's not by chance that you're in our midst on this day
And we hope through the entire service you will stay
Just let go and send up praises in Jesus name
Make up in your mind I won't leave here the way I came.

World Deliverance 3rd Anniversary Service
March 30 & April 1, 2001

BLACK HISTORY POEM

I once viewed a film entitled "Roots" written by Alex Haley
It showed how slaves were caught and sold daily
To prevent a slave from running they cut off his foot
Against their will the virginity of young women were took.

Prisoners held in bondage cried out to be free
This is not the life that was meant for you and me
In the beginning we were all created to be the same
To dislike someone because of their race is a shame.

Our ancestors were mistreated, beaten and killed
To many this remains to be a bitter pill
At some point in time we must let the past go
But never fail to share your history with everyone you know.

You can't take back what was taken away
But as "Fiddler" said, "there gon be another day"
Evil thoughts and deeds will he unfold
The secrets of all hearts will be told.

There is a purpose and a reason for each man's birth
The color of your skin should not determine your worth
Nor should it matter where you have or have not been
We all were shaped in iniquity and born in sin.

Take full advantage of the victories we have won
Acquaint yourself with the many inventions black historians have done
Don't take for granted the privilege to vote for the candidate of your choice
You are an American and you now have a voice.

The future no longer lies within any single person's hands
Your value is more than a mule and forty acres of land
One's diversity should be respected and appreciated by all
Be proud of your own heritage, speak out and stand tall.

2/19/04

Brenda A. Lasenby

CHRISTMAS TIME

Christmas is a time to celebrate our Savior's birth
A time to appreciate the Father for sending his son down to earth
A time to let go of the old and bring in the new
A time of refreshing, love and peace, just to name a few.

It's a special time for family and close friends
It's a time that let's us know the year is coming to an end
It's a time for reflecting, and a time for remembering too
Let us not get too busy and forget it's not about me or you.

A time to stop tearing down and to start building up
A time to seek after Christ the King, and ask him to fill our cup
It's a time to be happy, though some past memories tend to make us sad
Each year Christmas comes to remind us of all the happy ones we have had.

It's not about the many gifts you are going to receive
It's the time of year to offer prayer for those who are in need
All year long our many blessings we can count
Now is the time to help those that are down and out.

An expensive present you may not be able to buy
But we can be there to wipe someone's teary eyes
To say a kind word, to reach out, to give a gentle touch
The gift of caring is worth just as much.

There is not much time left to do what we have to do
The exact time of Christ's coming we really don't have a clue
Christmas time is just as good a time as any
To start claiming all the souls we will be winning.

It's a time to ask what can I do to help
A time to think of others and not just our self
It's a time to settle any and all feuds
It's a time to adopt a whole new attitude.

December 14, 2001

CREATION OF WOMAN

You are beautifully and wonderfully made according to the Father's will
You are bountifully blessed with wisdom and many skills
You have been adorned with gifts which man can not compete
It took the creation of Woman so that the male would be complete.

Know within yourself what it is you are to do
Know that no one else can accomplish this – only you
Equipped with everything that we need
Stop making excuses – accept the call and take heed.

We must take our position, move out and do our part
Now is the perfect time for us to start
Too long in the church we were not given our rightful place
In this day and time that is not the case.

The harvest is plenty but the laborers are few
The commandment to reach the lost was given for us too
No longer shall we sit and take a backseat
Feeling sorry for ourselves and claiming defeat.

I don't know about you, but I've been held down long enough
It is time to go forth and to show our stuff
I am tired of being fearful and afraid
The cost of my salvation has already been paid.

A foundation has been laid and Christ has opened up the way
What more is there for him to say?
Woman was not created to sit in the church and warm a pew
The question set before us is what are we here to do?

Brenda A. Lasenby

Dedication Day Prayer

We stand in awe seeing what the Father has done
The undertaking of this project was certainly not all fun
There was some murmuring, dissension and complaints
Yes, many which came directly from the saints.

No, it wasn't easy - he never said it would be
He simply vowed, I'll go with you, if you go with me
It's important to know what is written in the word
For by this knowledge our prayers are heard.

Christ fed five-thousand with two fish and five loaves
of bread. We are witnesses, he'll do just what he said
Let us strive on to carry this work out
Binding the spirit of fear, unbelief and doubt.

Wasn't Caleb sent to spy out the land?
Didn't Moses stretch out the rod that was in his hand?
Dear Lord, we're grateful for this your modern day servant man
He walked in obedience and carried out the master plan.

As we look around - we can see he gave us the best
A beautiful, comfortable place for our family, friends and guest
The vision is being unveiled even more and more
This ministry, like an eagle, is beginning to soar.

Though we know Pastor put everything he has on the line
Some of us **still** have doubts in our mind
If you look at the disbelieving faces the promises look dim
But **No man** can do these things, except God be with him.

Just as you were with Noah as he built the Ark
Lord, we thank you for being with us from the very start
Our instructions and directions were sent straight from you
With your guidance we knew exactly how and what to do.

When you have been given the "**go ahead**"
There may be some deep waters through which to tread
Seek after your goals with all your might
To come out victorious - you have to put up a fight.

Today we dedicate this edifice back to you
Your grace and your mercy made it possible to see it through
God took a little and made it much
Man within himself has never seen or heard of such.

There were those that thought we were heading for a fall
Many were afraid to leave **Behnan Hall**
But when the Lord speaks - it's time to pack-up and go
Abiding in his **Perfect Will** means you know - that you know -
that you know.

September 2, 2001

Brenda A. Lasenby

DIVINE EXPECTATION

While attending Summer Conference 2003
I claim victory and declare I will be set free
All my bondage will be left behind
I am here to receive what is mine.

The Father has enabled us to see another year
With love, power and a sound mind not of fear
This is my appointed time to be revived
God is not dead he's yet alive.

You have come for your hungry soul to be fed
Not of your own but by the spirit led
The table is spread – prepare for your spiritual meal
If you are sick in your body you can be healed.

We are expecting great and mighty things to come forth on this week
Men of faith and power are scheduled each night to speak
There will be heavenly singing seasoned to your taste
A word in a song could minister to your specific case.

You can have exactly what you say
On the altar all cares and burdens you may lay
The Lord listens to your every groan with open ears
He has seen the sleepless nights and the shed tears.

Don't leave this Conference without being changed
Expect to be different than you were when you came
You may have traveled from afar or perhaps you were near
Whatever the distance there's a blessing with your name on it here.

That problem you have been carrying and brought along
During Summer Conference look for it to be worked out and gone
Because where the presence of the Lord is the enemy cannot stay
He has to pack up and move on out of the way.

We are all in this together
Be it through sunshine or stormy weather
When we line up with the vision and are on one accord
Our prayers will bombard heaven and not be ignored.

Living in Divine Expectation is our theme
Every promise in the Word was meant for the redeemed
Just have the faith of a mustard seed to say so
The anointing will be released and the spirit will flow.

Brenda A. Lasenby

FOR THE HIGH SCHOOL GRADUATE

You have worked hard and have received your diploma
You are now an adult and not a child any longer
Love ones are more than happy to help with the decisions you must make
The rewards are endless in the opportunities you can take.

This is your beginning – high school days have come to an end
The true reality of the world is about to begin
Prepare yourself for disappointments for some will exist
Shun the presence of evil and you will never be amiss.

God has your future all in control
He alone is the keeper of your soul
Never would he bring you to this point to leave you alone
You can be kept no matter how far away from home.

Don't be afraid to go after your dreams
It does not matter how big they may seem
A child of the King you can pull rank
Take out of your vocabulary the words, "I can't".

Go out into the world and make your mark
Put your trust in God and you will know just where to start
Some may decide to marry taking a husband or wife
Just know the choices you select set the pattern for your life.

Apply your spiritual upbringing in the face of defeat
The author of adversity you will meet
Family and friends will not always be near
The voice of discouragement you will surely hear.

Loneliness and the feelings of failure you will have
With all that is within you a prayer reach up and grab
If and when your faith should ever fail
The Master will meet you like he met the woman at the well.

Whatever path you decide to venture down
Be determine for success I am bound
Walk in your own and not someone else's shoes
You can do all things through Christ which strengthens you.

June 11, 2002

GIVE THANKS

Lord we thank you for this Thanksgiving Day
You are a just God and you continue to make a way
Today is not just about turkey, dressing, yams and pies
But the one who protects us with his all seeing eyes.

Many families will bow their heads and say a prayer
Expressing gratitude for just being able to breathe fresh air
We have suffered a great attack upon our land
The future of our nation remains in your hands.

We seek your protection to keep hope alive
Help us not to fall prey to Satan and his lies
From you a wakeup call we have all received
Sometimes it takes this to put us on our knees.

Now that you have our attention and we know who is in control
The destiny of life and death only you can hold
You brought us into the world and you can take us out
This is reality and truth beyond all reasonable doubt.

Families across the nation gather to church services to give thanks
Business offices are closed as well as credit unions and banks
Enjoy the family dinners, the parades, and football games as they begin
Let us not revert to being unthankful when this Thanksgiving Day ends

November 15, 2001

GOD'S CHOSEN VESSEL

World Deliverance Temple is the place to be
For here God's anointing is flowing oh so free
It was in the plan of God to take our Pastor home
But didn't he promise he would never leave us along?

For over thirty years you stood close by the man of God's side
Never once were you lifted up in pride
There were many precious jewels entrusted in Pastor Miles' care
God loved his people too much not to treat them fair.

I have seen their disappointment and the tears that they have shed
I have chosen you so that they may continue to be fed
Therefore go forward my son in what I have called you to do
I am well able to take you through.

Don't take down for any devil in hell
For this cause I have prepared you well
Look not to the left neither to the right
Put your trust in God as you take your flight.

I promise never to lead you astray
But whatever you do - do it God's way
All your battles I promise I will fight
For I have called you out of darkness
into my marvelous light.

Saints of WDT let us forever hold Pastor Ferguson up in prayer
Don't be a benchwarmer one that just sits and stare
We are here to work and not to play
For our time is not tomorrow it is today.

15

Brenda A. Lasenby

GOD'S STATUE OF A MAN

A creation after God's own heart
You made a vow you would never let him part
You gave up all to follow him
You refused to take down at every whim.

He has been by your side all the way
Keeping you with the victory both night and day
Your tears of sadness and times of sorrow he has seen
Our Savior's eyes are oh so keen.

Many have come and many have went
I'm sure you realize all those people were not sent
Perhaps to hinder the work is why they came
But found you were not interested in playing a game.

There is nothing when you ask in faith he won't do
God has proven himself and has always brought you through
He promised to make you the head and not the tail
Take hold of his word for you know he cannot fail.

Another prosperous year has passed
Even though some said you would not last
With much dignity hold your head up high
For we that are ready will meet him in the sky.

Continue to lead and set God's people free
You are his chosen vessel and always will be
When you have done all to stand – just stand
For you are God's Statute of a Man.

Written for Apostle Charles O. Miles

GRADUATE'S INSPIRATION

Whether you have just graduated from high school or college
You have now obtained a higher level of knowledge
Graduation is a different and exciting experience in your life
Some decisions you make will be wrong and some will be right.

The journey you travel will be challenging and brand new
God has a bright future already planned just for you
How many times have you been asked, "what do you want to be?"
Whatever you may chose - Jesus let them always see.

You may decide to continue on and pursue additional training
Or acquire that perfect job for which you have been aiming
Whatever path at this point you makeup in your mind to take
Be open and be prayerful in the decisions that you make.

As you move forward into your new role
Many adventures will began to unfold
This Day of Celebration will soon be a day in your past
A long time coming but it's over so fast.

Take the Lord along with you everywhere you go
He wants to be near you more than you will ever know
If you remember to always let him be first
Your steps will be blessed and not cursed.

Pastor, Sis. Ferguson and WDT are so proud of you
Your Mom, your Dad and your family are too
As you walk out and walk into your new phase
Be sure to give God the glory, the honor and the praise.

For without him this day would not have come about
It took a lot of prayers to successfully get you out
Now go on and strive to be all you can be
It is written nothing is impossible with me.

6/18/01

HAPPY BIRTHDAY

Happy Birthday to the Greatest Mom in the world
With this family you are our #1 Girl
We appreciate every second, minute and hour that we share
Your love, guidance and expertise are always there.

You are sweet, gentle, kind and we hold you so dear
Grateful to celebrate your birthday with you another year
You have been blessed to have your health and strength renewed
You still enjoy shopping for those new hats, dresses and shoes.

When we were young you saw to it that food was on the table
Many things you desired for us but you were not financially able
Our Christmas holiday was always a very happy affair
Peeking under the beds at our gifts? Some did not dare.

We enjoy spending time with you and for your attention we don't fight
You have enough love for your husband, sons, daughter and grandchildren alike
You make us all feel special in your own unique way
When we come to visit we are so comfortable we want to stay.

You have been a marriage counselor when there were problems with our mates
You told us to hang in there when there were things we said we couldn't take
You have always guided us with wisdom in the right direction
Yet you never hesitated to apply the necessary correction.

We are who we are today because of you
Your life has not been easy – you have really been through
You didn't take down and in self pity wallow
But you stood strong as an example for others to follow.

(8/5/03)

HE LIVES

What more can Jesus, the Son of God do
He suffered, bled and died on the cross for you
The price was paid way back on calvary
Just so all mankind could be free.

His accusers could have saved him by choosing Barabbus to die
But it was the Father's will for his only son to be crucified
Christ's suffering was for our guilt and shame
Had he not given his life it would not have been the same.

He hung on the cross and didn't say a mumbling word
The weeping of his mother, Mary, could loudly be heard
If it be possible let this cup pass from me he prayed
The transgressions of the world on him were laid.

On that third day he got up with all power in his hands
Neither death nor the grave could hold the man
The disobedience of the first human creation put us in sin
But a way was made so that we could live again.

(Written for Easter, 2003)

Brenda A. Lasenby

HOLY WOMAN IN BATTLE

We are soldiers on the battlefield
Our purpose is to do the Master's will
The helmet of salvation is upon our head
Many are hungry and waiting to be fed.

God's command is to bring the lost souls in
To bind the enemy and set them free from sin
We won't bend and we won't bow
For one day we made the Lord a vow.

We have the strength, we have the power
We have been chosen for this very hour
War has been declared upon Satan and his pact
We're ready to snatch every soul back.

We are more than conquerors devil
In God we are moving to another level
Holy women in battle on the front line
Be bold, be strong, there's not much time.

Fast, witness, seek God and pray
These things we must do each and every day
We will win this battle – I know we can
Just keep your hand in his hand.

Some things in this battle it takes a Holy Woman to do
A part of God's plan was made especially for you
So let us not be weary in well doing and don't faint
A crown of life is waiting for every saint.

September 26, 1999
(Women's Day Service – Sunday)

IN SPITE OF

What is there in my existence that attempts to hold me down?
Why do you approach me with uncertainty and frowns?
In spite of negative opinions I press on toward the mark
A ray of sunshine has delivered me from the dark.

I continue to progress in spite of your disbelief
I have been successful though you caused me much grief
Determination overpowers defeat to make me strong
All failures will be used as giant stepping stones.

In the face of adversity learn to encourage yourself
Be responsible for your own actions and no one else
When you lack commitment from others do it on your own
Some things are better done when you do them alone.

I realize the power that lies within the tongue
It is a weapon used that is as dangerous as a gun
In spite of discouraging words spoken strive to achieve
Stand firm in the faith and hold on to what you believe.

(8/27/03)

IT'S YOUR TIME

Oh taste and see that the Lord is good
For he has blessed this ministry like no one else could
I know at times you felt all alone
But the Father was watching from his throne.

God has honored you for your firm stand
And commanded that you go forth and spy out the land
Old slew-foot thought he had you down
But let no man take away your crown.

Though right now you may in number be few
You know what you have been called out to do
So don't you worry and don't you fret
Has God ever failed you yet?

Being fulfilled is what was prophesied many years ago
That from this place Deliverance would flow
People will be coming with many needs
As a servant of the Almighty their souls you must feed.

Every knee must bow and every tongue confess
Because you stood by the ministry today is your day to be blessed
Now we know some were chosen and some were sent
But Pastor and Sis. Thomas were ordained to be right here in Flint.

It's your time now I heard the Father say
There is no longer any time to delay
My coming is soon and it is sure
Reach the people while their hearts are pure.

The anointing is encamped around your fold
Don't be afraid to step out in God and be bold
As long as your steps are in his will
It won't be long this place will be filled.
Know that he's forever standing right by your side
As long as in him you continue to abide.

Dedicated to Pastor John & Eileen Thomas

JUST FOR YOU

We Welcome Ma Winans, a woman of beauty,
charm and grace. We count it a privilege as well
as a blessing to have her in this place.
Though I've never met you face to face
I know that on Christ the solid rock your
life is based.

A sweet, seasoned, holy woman of God
One who certainly knows about not sparing the rod.
A perfect example of how rearing children should be done
Ma and Pa Winans are the proud parents of three girls and
seven sons.

A Mother of children who possess fortune and fame
Ma Winans taught living holy was not a game
Back in the day we were told it was either heaven or hell
It was this message that enabled her children to turn out so well.

Early in life she knew her offspring were gifted
And prayed, Lord into the enemy's hands don't let
them be sifted. An example in the home all parents
should be. A child is the product of their environment you see.

All have been touched and inspired by the lyrics the
Winans family sings. Today we say thank you for not
selling out for material things.

Ma Winans will walk through many open doors
The spirit of the Lord is going to use her like never before
As she ministers in song, teach or preach
Heaven only knows how many souls she will reach.

.

Brenda A. Lasenby

We await with anticipation to receive the word
With appreciation that you came here to serve
Feel free to let the Lord use you in his own way
Give to us whatever it is he has told you to say.

In Honor of Ma Winans
at WDT - August 12, 2001

LIFE ANEW

As we begin our life anew
Let us not dwell on who was at fault – me or you
We're going to dismiss all negative forces of the past
As we prepare to make our marriage last.

This is not to say problems we won't face
But we will deal with them at a much slower pace
Together as a family we must strive to rebuild what was torn down
The gleam of happiness will replace the frown.

The truth is that we have all learned a lot
For survival a relationship must be built upon a solid rock
We have now come into a new realization
The storms of life will indeed uproot your foundation.

No longer will we walk as being two
From this day on we shall rejoice for what God has taken us through
One in the spirit and one in mind
Together as one we shall forever bind.

(4/14/97)

Men Should Always Pray And Not Faint

What are we to do as a saint?
Men ought to always pray and not faint
His promises to you are yea and not nay
On your face in prayer you must lay.

The key of faith will unlock any door
Make your request known - don't beg anymore
Men ought to always pray and not faint
We serve a God who never says, "I can't."

Your provisions have already been made
If only we realized the price Christ has paid
With open arms he waits to converse with you
Concerned about whatever it is you're going through.

Prayer will bring back to life that which was dead
Your spiritual man is hungry and begs to be fed
Talk to me - tell me what it is that you need
You will reap in due time if you sow good seed.

The effectual fervent prayers of a righteous man availeth much
If you want to hear from heaven - you have to keep in touch
God the Father and Jesus are one
For you he gave his only begotten son.

Have I not proven myself time and time again?
Yet you cease to pray and let the enemy come in
Men should always pray and not faint
Don't be deceived by the false pictures he paints.

Satan will show you great riches and say you can have it all
But know that you are being set-up for a fall
Daniel was cast down deep into the lion's den
Prayer was the answer even way back then.

What it took in the Bible days - is what it takes now
Stand before your giant - refuse to bend or bow
Men should always pray and not faint
He didn't teach you to swim -- to let you sank.

Prayer Breakfast - April 20, 2002

Brenda A. Lasenby

MOTHER'S DAY LUNCHEON WELCOME

Welcome to World Deliverance Temple Mother's Day Luncheon
We are happy you are here to participate in this Women of Charity function
The money you paid for a ticket has been well spent
This afternoon will consist of several exciting events.

Our WDT Fashion Show is a prime example
The beautiful garments that will be modeled is just a sample
There was a lot of work and planning done especially for our guests
The menu of fine foods prepared will be some of the best.

Because we are save does not mean we can't have a good time
This program has been designed especially with you in mind
So sit back, relax and enjoy yourself - - you deserve a lift
You might be chosen to win one of the lovely gifts!

I don't know who extended the invitation for you to come
It may have been a wife, a husband, a father, a daughter or a son
Please feel free to walk around, be sociable, and visit the other tables
If you don't know someone - just check out their name label.

We're here together to have some laughs and a little fun
Try and forget about the things we left behind that need to be done
For certain they will be there when you leave and go home
You'll still have time to wash the dishes, to scrub and shine the chrome.

We are gathered today to show all "Mothers" some love
For they are our guardian angels sent from heaven above
A Mother will travel down the road with you to the last mile
No matter how you act or what you do - you are still her child.

May 2, 2003

"MOTHERS"
God's Precious Gift

In the beginning God created
Man in the image of himself
He created Mothers to be of help
Someone wise, virtuous and strong
Someone to teach us right from wrong.

Your precious gift of a Mother
You gave to every one
All your works are so miraculously done
Each Mother is given responsibility
To care for her own child
A Mother is a precious gift from heaven
Loaned to us for only a while.

At birth your life she begins to pave
You can never count the many sacrifices she has made
A Mother leads, shelters, protects and lends a smile
Her love will go with you to the last mile.

Sons and daughters shaped in iniquity and born in sin
It's usually Mother who shows us how we can win
Praying and bringing the strong holds of Satan down
Leading her children on to victory to receive their crown.

She teaches us patience and how to endure
A Mother's love is sweet and oh so pure
Her wisdom and knowledge we hold so dear
But chastisement and instructions we must hear.

Without ever telling -- your problems she sees
A Mother finds answers by staying on her knees
There is no charge -- this gift is yours with his love
Your own precious **"Mother"** -- sent from God above.

Brenda A. Lasenby

MY HOPE

My hope is that our lives have been changed
We have caused each other more than enough pain
There are some things in life that are destined to be
Such as what happened between you and me.

My hope is that together we will rebuild our relationship
To always be conscious of the words that we speak from our lips
We cannot take back angry words once they are spoken
This results in the lines of communication being broken.

My hope extends far beyond the material things we have lost
For all those things in time can once again be bought
My hope is for the unity and love we pledged many years ago
That feeling of having my very own hero.

My hope today is also our hope for tomorrow
True happiness is not something you can borrow
My hope for the present and future is what I have described
A hope of love, joy and peace to be fulfilled forever in our lives.

1/29/98

OUR FIRST LADY

Our First Lady was born and set aside for such a time as this
Had Pastor not obeyed just look at what he would have missed
A vessel chosen to stand by the man of God's side
Yet possessing the knowledge and wisdom in her own gifts to abide.

Always ready and willing to lend a helping hand
She never waivers from taking a firm stand
Obedient and attentive to the Lord's will
Our First Lady has a work to fulfill.

Over time you were being prepared and being taught
Learning how to put on the whole armor for the battles to be fought
Little did you know what was in God's plan
When he blessed you with such a fine young man.

Some may say your standards are old-fashion and a bit out of date
Bur Our First Lady's goal is to reach the pearly gate
A woman of love, patience and such a beautiful smile
This First Lady has her own style.

Her life in Christ has been fully hid
She is devoted to her husband and her kids
Our First Lady will help you in any way she can
If you mean to do right she'll be your biggest fan.

You have walked with the Master for a long time
All it took was a made-up mind
On this journey down through the years
Our First Lady has shed many tears.

Yet standing steadfast, faithful and true
A living testimony that the Savior brought her through
Never a murmur nor a complaint
Our First Lady is a genuine saint.

Brenda A. Lasenby

Blessed to live another year
Spread the news that Christ's coming is near
Teach the young women to be better wives
How to be fulfilled in every area of their lives.

Our First Lady has been tried in the fire
Being used by God is her earnest desire
A solider battling against the enemy of sin
Be encouraged and go forth in the capacity you are in.

Dedicated to Evangelist Delores Ferguson
2/28/01

In Appreciation to Pastor Ferguson's Retirement

His initial employment began by washing the executives cars
His final position as Engineering Manager exceeded that by far
Climbing the corporate ladder can really be tough
To reach a higher level - you have to know your stuff.

In order to succeed, to a certain extent, you must be meek
This is one of several qualifications that the Boss Man seeks
The fine qualities that you portrayed as an Evangelist out on the field
Were the same ones that convinced Ford Motor Company you "fit the bill".

A born Leader in the spiritual realm as well as in the natural too
You were chosen by Ford because you knew what to do
A man of distinction, with zeal, ability and wisdom
One who was not discouraged nor afraid to challenge the system.

He was on a mission seeking how to better himself
Searching security for his family - not self wealth
I see him as a Shepherd watching over his flock
Some have seen him as an executive protecting
the company's bonds and stock.

In whatever role Roy Ferguson may have played in your life
You must agree he has always been honest, kind and upright
Employed by Ford Motor Company for thirty-four long years
He is greatly respected by his family and all his peers.

The capable and gifted leadership abilities you possess
Are in no way about to be put to rest
Those abilities within our church are already being used
It's those capabilities that are going to fill up our pews.

Though your tenure with Visteon may have come to an end
A whole new adventure is about to begin
To these, your fellow co-workers you must depart
Your commission to the "full time" ministry is just beginning to start.

Brenda A. Lasenby

Today we see a different path you have been called out to take
This retirement won't be spent just sitting out on the lake
Even though at times you may have had to swallow bitter pills
Continue to lead using your God-given skills.

Where fate will take you now it does not yet appear
Just continue to keep your mind open - listening with an attentive ear
You have paid your dues and came up through the ranks
For this we extend our honor, our appreciation, and our thanks.

Praise Belongs to God

Five years ago Roy D. Ferguson answered the Pastoral call
He caught and obeyed the vision to leave Behnan Hall
God ordained and equipped him to be the man
Many of us did not agree nor did we understand.

Sometimes the will of God may not be what we have planned
The direction for our lives is solely in his hands
When he decided the Apostle had finished his course and ran a good race
He chose one of his servants to be the Pastor in this place.

While seeking the Lord's guidance as to how to put it together
He had to endure some cloudy and some stormy weather
God is not slack concerning the promises he has made
A way will be opened and the foundation firmly laid.

International Deliverance Tabernacle was our initial name
Upon entering this new home World Deliverance Temple is who we became
Many joined this church proclaiming they were God sent
But when things didn't go their way they packed up and went.

We could not have accomplished what you see here on our own
This consist of more than just the labor of flesh and bones
Blind faith had to be exercised and put into a course of action
Claiming the outcome to be victorious with full satisfaction.

No single person can take the credit for what has been done
At times we faced deadlines that put us all under the gun
Praise Belongs to God is our 5th Anniversary theme
For on him and him alone we did lean.

Those standing with this ministry are being blessed
The negative force fighting against us is only a test
Don't worry if some are being indifferent and bold
God has the situation all in control.

Brenda A. Lasenby

We are taught in this ministry to walk according to the word
We have been encouraged by what our ears have heard
We offer a full spiritual menu serving whatever you need
We have a real leader that came from good seed.

We shall continue walking by faith and not by sight
In just a little while the wrong will be made right
Come and sit on the services if you wish
The presence of the Lord is still moving in our midst.

WDT is a growing church that is on the move
Whatever gift you possess here it can be used
My personal testimony is that my spirit has been revived
God said for us to live and not to die.

The Diversity of God

Why is it that we can not live together as one?
It was for each of us that God gave his only son
It should matter less rather you're red, black or white
We are his children and we are precious in his sight.

Our goals, our ambitions, they are similar if not the same
The final destiny for us is to return to the dust from whence we came
We were born into the world and created to be equal by God
Then man came along and presented his own false facade.

Man is diverse and come in various sizes, shapes and colors
Yet he has been commanded to love one another
Being of a different origin is not so bad
If we looked and acted the same that would be truly sad.

The creation of man is a miracle within itself
Be who you are and not a carbon copy of someone else
Stand tall and represent whatever your ancestors stood for
They have suffered and have opened a many door.

Take the time to explore and understand the diversities
of what your culture might be
Know that the same God in his infinite love
that made you is the same God that made me.

The death of God's son was not based upon your nationality or race
He died that we may one day see him face to face
They stretched him wide and hung him on a tree
Christ gave up his life so that we could be free.

Let us tear down those built-up barrier walls
Freedom and the pursuit of happiness exists for us all
Come on my brother, and my sister, give me your hand
Together as one we will make it to the Promised Land.

2/4/02

Brenda A. Lasenby

THE GIFT OF CHRISTMAS

The Gift of Christmas wrapped in swaddling clothes
Laying in the manger for all to behold
There was no room for him in the inn
His birth was to deliver the world from sin.

Three Wise Men traveled from afar
They were told to follow the star
The Gift of Life come and see
Worship him on bending knee.

Hark the Herald Angel sings
Glory and Honor to the newborn king
The Gift of Hope and the Gift of Love
Sent all the way down from heaven above.

Receive the Gift of Christmas that was given to us all
Take heed when you hear the Master's call
His Gift is not lying in the manger anymore
But seeking to enter into every open door.

We offer up to you the sacrifice of praise
With our hearts opened and our hands raised
Thank you God for the Gift of Jesus your son
Without him we would be lost and undone.

Let us remember this holiday season
Jesus is the purpose and he is the reason
With trees and decorations your home you may adorn
But spread the word that the Savior is born!

(12/8/2003)

THE MAN FOR THIS HOUR

The Man for this hour
Has been endowed with spiritual power
He has been planted and must bloom in this place
He can't be moved by the looks on your face.

This Man of God has nothing to hide
His life in Christ is where he abides
He is not going to tell you anything wrong
His orders come straight from the throne.

Because he is the Shepherd chosen to watch over this flock
The work of the Lord will not be stopped
Laboring day and night for his sheep
Praying, fasting and waiting on answers while we sleep.

Your best interest he always has in mind
A man of God, he's gentle and he's kind
Now many of us were sad, down and out
But we now have new joy, a dance and a shout.

We all know from whence we came
Some were wounded and some were lame
Come on Saints let the spirit of the Lord flow
Even mightier miracles to us the Lord will show.

As we increase in number by leaps and bounds
Word of this ministry will spread around
People will come from the East, West, North and South
Many just to see what we are all about.

Let us not worry who might come and who might go
Just know in your heart that this work will grow
As we listen with anticipation to each and every sermon
Always remember we're older, wiser, stronger and more
determined.

3/29/01

Brenda A. Lasenby

"The Spirit of Christmas"

The **Spirit of Christmas** is in the air
People showing kindness is not at all rare
The purpose of the season is to rejoice over the Savior's birth
For he came all the way down from heaven to earth.

What can I do to let my light shine
We should endeavor to everyday be kind
The **Spirit of Christmas** is not just about one day
The shining star from Bethlehem showed us the way.

The Gift of Christmas was given without any charge
He came wrapped in swaddling clothes and he wasn't very large
Though there was no room for him in the inn
He's knocking at the door of our hearts again.

He's not that little baby laying in the manger anymore
He's Lord and King whom we love and adore
His holy conception should always within us abide
He is our strong tower, our shield and our guide.

Would you have offered up your only begotten son?
The Father cared so much - this is what he has done
The **Spirit of Christmas** was displayed a long time ago
A plan was designed because he loved us so.

Don't let Christ's birthday be in vain
Not to take advantage of his arrival would be ashame
Let the **Spirit of Christmas** live within your very soul
Bring someone that has lost their way into the fold.

Nothing in life for granted we should take
It is a blessing to go to sleep and each morning to awake
I am most grateful for having my mother here
To celebrate Christmas with our family this year.

For she was attacked by the enemy with a stroke
He set out to destroy her - it was no joke
But strength is yet being administered from on high
It is declared she shall live and not die.

So show compassion in what others are going through
For tomorrow, who knows - it could possibly be you
Let the **Spirit of Christmas** always be near
Take every opportunity to spread holiday cheer.

(12/12/02)

Brenda A. Lasenby

THESE KIND ARE IN THE CHURCH

Usually one of the first walking through the door
They unresponsively react as it it's all a bore
Feeling that there has been a personal assignment of seats
If someone else happens to sit there – you can feel the heat
Not here for the purpose of doing any kind of work
These kind are in the Church.

Speaking and spreading lies out of their mouth
They have lost their joy and their shout
Can't wait until it's time to dismiss and go home
They rush out so they can gossip on the telephone
Looking for the negative in what the Lord has birthed
These kind are in the Church.

While in your presence they smile in your face
But when you're not around they are on your case
They don't like the sermons you come on too strong
No matter what you preach they find something wrong
Sitting on the pew inattentive, half asleep and not alert
These kind are in the Church.

Dissatisfied with the way things are going
They say and do that which is so annoying
When programs are put on they never play an active part
Instead they show how much dissension they can start
Much pleasure is received when others are being hurt
These kind are in the Church.

Their heart has become hardened and seldom do they weep
It is very unusual if you see them twice in a week
Never feeling the need to answer the altar call
Without a change they are headed for a fall
You may be wondering, "Where do these kind of people lurk?"
These kind are in the Church.

Nothing that is heard is getting through
But if they don't want help there is nothing you can do
Living and existing in a dangerous state of mind
Soon they will run out of time
Their spiritual condition is now even worse
These kind are in the Church.

Will you rob God is the question at hand
His spirit will not always strive with man
When they are upset their tithes and offerings you won't see
In need of deliverance – you may as well let them be
Somewhat uncomfortable another ministry they begin to search
These kind are in the Church.

1/28/03

Brenda A. Lasenby

WE HAVE COME THUS FAR

Just look around at what God has done
He has blessed us each and everyone
It was said that the vision would not come to pass
There were some that felt Pastor was moving too fast.

We have come thus far and even further we will go
For God is not finished with this vision you know
He is preparing to bring the people in and to set them free
His word is true and there is so much more for us to see.

I am ready and I am willing to follow this journey through
Let us get excited about what the Lord is going to do
He has already proven himself in so many ways
There is more to come in just a matter of days.

We have come thus far trusting in his holy word
The saints have a manifold of blessings yet unheard
He brought us out but only to bring us in
A new existence, a new start, a new life free from sin.

We are on our way now to bigger and better things
The blessed, the prosperous, the children of a king
Look not back at what use to be
Unlock closed doors with our God given key.

We have prayed, we have fasted and we have waited
To many saints this procedure is outdated
By faith we have come thus far
We know what our real weapons are.

Run with the vision be sure to make it plain
For we have hell to shun and heaven to gain
We have come thus far and further we shall go
Thanks be to God from whom all blessings flow.

12/21/2000

"WE MADE IT"

The Choir is not here to put on a show
But through the ministry of singing to let us know
There is salvation, healing and deliverance in his wings
Your needs can be met by the songs they will sing
Let the melody and the lyrics minister unto your inner man
A good anointed chorus will do what nothing else can.

Now for some it may take a song with a fast beat
Just to make you clap your hands and get up off your seat
No matter what your style of music may be
You are in for a blessing just you wait and see
The Choir has fasted and the Choir has prayed
Many late nights in rehearsal they have stayed.

WDT Inspirational Choir lift up your voices and sing the power down
We have made it thus far and nothing will turn us around
When God is in a thing it simply has to work
Being a child of the King certainly has its perks
What the cankerworm thought he had snatched away
Was replaced with hope and a brighter day.

Though in your infancy you may have been small in number
It wasn't long before others desired to become a member
At times your way may look cloudy and dim
Whatever you do keep your focus on him
Instill words of praises on your tongue
Within your heart always have a song.

Each one of you are as a precious gem
Functioning not in yourself but in the spirit rim
Oh make a joyful noise unto the Lord
Give him glory with every chord
There is no secret what God can do
With his help – we made it through

Many thought the enemy had us licked
But look at us now -- We Made It!

Brenda A. Lasenby

We feel the presence of the Lord in this Anniversary tonight
For we walk by faith and not by sight
The lies that were told didn't bother us one bit
With our old folks and our little children -- We Made It!

4th WDT Choir Anniversary, 10/2002

WEAPON OF PRAYER

Prayer is the sincere desires of the heart
Prayer is how each day should start
Whisper a prayer in the morning, noon and night
Pray that everything will turn out right.

Come boldly to the throne of grace
Run with patience this Christian race
Your Prayers should never cease
The Chains of Bondage God will release.

Pray when you're up - Pray when you're feeling down
Though you might not see him - the Devil is always around
We have been given a strong weapon with which to fight
When used forcibly the results are out of sight!

Though we suffer persecution and strife
The Creator is in control of our life
All he wants us to do is Pray
Talking with him will keep the enemy away.

Man should always Pray and never faint
A Prayer Life should dwell in every saint
Pray Until Something Happens - your situation
can not remain the same
Pray Until Something Happens
Claim the victory in Jesus name!

You don't have to say a lot of pretty words
For even your faintest groan he has heard
Prayer will take out of you that which shouldn't be in
A contrite and broken spirit Prayer will mend.

Now Faith will move a mountain and
Prayer will unlock closed doors
Just ask and believe it -- the Answers
are already yours.

Brenda A. Lasenby

Don't worry about being down on bending knees
Sit-up, lie down -- use whatever position you please
The main objective is to get the Prayer through
The method used is entirely up to you.

April 27, 2001
[Prayer Breakfast 5/5/01]

WHERE DO WE GO FROM HERE?

Where do we go from here?
That is my greatest fear
How to put it together again?
Or if we even can.

Some say starting all over is not so bad
But it is painful to think about what you once had
Lord, please show us the way
Lead and guide us each and every day.

Help us to be completely in your will
To be able to just stand still
Give us the plan you would have us to use
If we are in your will we will not be confused.

Where do we go from here?
Please make your directions
perfectly clear.

Brenda A. Lasenby

WHY DON'T YOU HEAR?

I talk and talk but you don't hear
Everything that is said goes beyond your ears
You see me with your natural eyes
But your thoughts are far away in the skies.

You must ask God to be your guide
To help you not to believe so many lies
The truth one day will be unsealed
The secrets of all hearts will then be revealed.

I talk and talk, but you don't hear
I've tried to tell you my many fears
There are many things we must do
Just to see this relationship through.

You and I we can't do it alone
It will take he who sits on the throne
Please know that you and I have so much to learn
Yes, quite a bit before you can expect me to return.

(3/1/4/97)

WHY?

God is one who does all things well
Why he does these things he never has to tell
I know I am not the only one pondering in their mind
Lord, why did it have to be Pastor's time?

We seem to have forgotten you loaned him to us for only awhile
We leaned so heavily on him to help us with our trials
A lesson is learned in everything that you do
Even with the sting of death you are able to carry us through.

Please help me not to question your will
But give me the grace and the wisdom to be still
My greatest concern while dealing with the pain
I don't want Pastor's labor to be in vain.
We have to strive hard each day to put up a good fight
We too must be ready when God calls us to take our flight.

10/13/97
(A Dedication to Apostle Charles O. Miles)

Brenda A. Lasenby

WOMEN

As Women we have roles we are required to play
One is to teach our family how important it is to pray
For when we are within ourselves totally set free
We can show others where it is they should be.

Within the Body of Christ Women contribute an important part
We usually have a "knack" of how to do things from the start
Yet we can line-up with the program and know how to follow
In being submissive sometimes our pride we have to swallow.

No, we may not always do everything just right
But we tackle difficult situations with all our might
Persistence is a virtue that most Women possess
Determined through adversity to do their very best.

According to the scripture Women are the weaker vessel
But it does not say this makes her any lesser
So standing tall in the sight of God she takes her rightful place
She arms herself with whatever is needed to run this Christian race.

We have attended and enjoyed this Women's Retreat
We went in with an attitude to conquer and to defeat
Many arrived with needs they wanted to be met
Crying out with lifted hands to receive all they could get.

What God has begun he will finish
His word will stand and never be diminished
All his beginnings also have an end
He completes that which he begins.

To those that gave up fully and left the pass behind
You have the testimony I received what was mine
Much was accomplished in the two days that we were gone
When you come with expectancy it don't take long.

So we return to our respective homes declaring not to be the same
A change has taken place in our lives and total victory obtained
Walk in new liberty and be not entangled by the enemy's yoke
Keep your eyes on the prize and don't worry about folks.

Women's Retreat
9/9/03

Brenda A. Lasenby

WORLD DELIVERANCE TEMPLE
SUMMER CONFERENCE 2002 WELCOME

World Deliverance Temple extends a warm welcome to "Summer Conference 2002
Our Pastor, Co-Pastor and congregation are so happy to see each one of you
Realizing that a lot of churches were passed while coming this way
We say, "thank you" for choosing to worship with us today.

We sincerely promise that your coming will not be in vain
Blessings are being disbursed and one is inscribed with your name
Attendance at this Summer Conference is not just by chance
You are in the divine will of God and your life will be enhanced.

Make yourself comfortable, sit back and kick off your shoes
Listen attentively as the minister delivers the gospel of good news
Please accept this invitation to welcome the Lord in
Let loose and let God do it for you all over again.

I know you felt the presence of the Lord as you entered the door
He wants to give you the testimony, "I won't be the same anymore."
Those old burdens that you are carrying – refuse to take them back home
Turn them all over to him – you are not in this battle alone.

Feel free to sing, jump, dance and shout giving God glory and praise
As you stand in the sanctuary with your hearts lifted up and hands raised
The spirit of discouragement, loneliness, poverty, and unbelief we bind
Tell the devil what God has for me in this Conference is already mine.

Now we must inform you that the program is subject to change
Our order of service may not every night be the same
But there is another important factor you should also know
In whatever direction the Holy Ghost leads us – that's the way we will go!

(7/18/02)

ABOUT THE AUTHOR

Brenda A. Lasenby was born on August 11, 1949 to Carrie and Loade Johnson in Ecorse, Michigan. She has five brothers, Loade, Jr., Sylvester (deceased) Jimmy, Donell and Dr. Jerry Johnson. Brenda has been married to Robert Lasenby for thirty-one years and they reside in West Bloomfield, Michigan. Brenda and Robert are the parents of two sons, Shane Kwan, DeJuan Antonio, and the grandparents of a beautiful granddaughter, Shayla Breann.

A member of World Deliverance Temple (WDT) in Dearborn Heights, Michigan since its inception in March of 1999, Brenda serves as Secretary of the Executive Governing Board. Her Pastor is Bishop Roy D. Ferguson and her Co-Pastor is Evangelist Delores Ferguson. Prior to becoming a member of WDT, Brenda attended International Gospel Center in Ecorse, Michigan for approximately thirty-eight years under the leadership of the late Apostle Charles O. Miles. Under direction and auspice of Apostle Miles, Brenda received "old-fashion" teaching. This caliber of teaching equipped her with the necessary knowledge needed to maintain a firm and solid spiritual foundation. Brenda dedicated her life to the Lord at the age of twelve years old and has the testimony that God can keep you if you want to be kept.

Printed in the United States
153860LV00004B/19/A